THE SINGER

Calvin Miller

D1125193

InterVarsity Press
Downers Grove
Illinois 60515

© 1975 by Inter-Varsity Christian Fellowship of the United States of America.

All rights reserved. No part of this book may be reproduced in any form without written permission from InterVarsity Press.

InterVarsity Press is the book-publishing division of Inter-Varsity Christian Fellowship.

Distributed in Canada through InterVarsity Press, 1875 Leslie St., Unit 10, Don Mills, Ontario M3B 2M5, Canada.

ISBN Cloth: 0-87784-871-8
ISBN Paper: 0-87784-639-1
Library of Congress Catalog Card Number: 74-20097

Printed in the United States of America

23	22	21	20	19	18	17	16	15	
89	88	87	86	85	84	83	82	81	80

I

For most who live,
hell is never knowing
who they are.
The Singer knew and
knowing was his torment.

When he awoke, the song was there.

Its melody beckoned and begged him to sing it.

It hung upon the wind and settled in the meadows where he walked.

He knew its lovely words and could have sung it all, but feared to sing a song whose harmony was far too perfect for human ear to understand.

And still at midnight it stirred him to awareness, and with its haunting melody it drew him with a curious mystery to stand before an open window.

In rhapsody it played among the stars.

It rippled through Andromeda and deepened Vega's hues.

It swirled in heavy strains from galaxy to galaxy and gave him back his very fingerprint.

"Sing the Song!" the heavens seemed to cry. "We never could have been without the melody that you alone can sing."

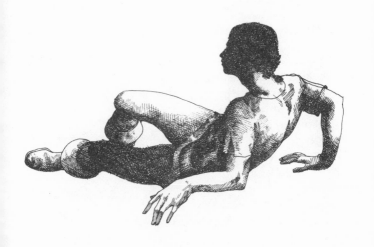

But he drew back, sighing
that the song they so
desired was higher than the earth.

And always in his agony of
longing and reluctance, the
atmosphere around him argued
back.

"You, too, are higher than the
earth! You sang the higher
music once, before the oceans
ever crashed their craggy
coasts."

He braced himself upon a
precipice above the canyon floor,
and with the wind full on his
face, he cried into the sky:

"Earthmaker, tell me
if I have the right
to sing..."

But then his final word trailed
off into gales.

The gull screamed.

"No," he thought, "only Earth-
maker is everlasting. His
alone must be the theme from
which sprung the world I
stand upon."

And so he only loved but never
sang the song.

Full well he knew that few
would ever see him as a singer

of so grand a piece.

He knew that they would say to
him:

"You are no singer! And even
if you are you should sing the
songs we know."

And well he knew the penalty of
law. A dreamer could be ostracized
in hate for singing songs the
world had never heard.

Such songs had sent a thousand
singers to their death already.

And the song which dogged his
aching steps and begged him
pleadingly to sing it was
completely unfamiliar.

Only the stars and mountains
knew it. But they were old. And
man was new, and chained to
simple, useless rhymes; thus he
could not understand the majesty
that settled down upon him.

But daily now it played upon his
heart and swept his soul, until
the joy exploded his awareness—
crying near the edge of sanity,
"Sing... sing... S I N G!"

¶¶

It is strange how
oftentimes the air
speaks.

We are sane as long
as we hear voices
when there are none.

We are insane when
we hear nothing and
worse we are deaf.

He worked the wood and drove
the pegs methodically.

The shavings from the adze
piled high upon the floor.

"Earthmaker, full of mercy,"
he said, when evening had
come, "I am a tradesman!"

"No," said the silent air,
"not a tradesman—a troubadour instead!"

"A tradesman!" he said firmly
as he smashed his mallet on
the vise.

"A troubadour!" the silence
thundered back.

III

Two artists met one time within
a little wood. Each brought
his finest painting stroked by
his complete uniqueness. When
each revealed his canvas to the
other—they were identical.

So once in every solar system
there are two fingerprints alike.

But only once.

His seeming madness made the
music play a hundred times
more loudly than before.

It lured him from his highland
home.

He left the mallet broken on
the vise and walked away.

Never had he been the way he
walked, and yet his feet knew
every step. He could not cease
to marvel how they moved his
body forward through the
mist of circumstances which he
vaguely knew by name.

His naked feet intrigued him,
for they moved with purpose
which his mind had not yet
measured. Besides they each
one wore a curious scar of some
wound as yet unopened; yet they
had been there long before his
birth. What twist of meaning
had Earthmaker given him, to
scar his feet before he ever
walked?

From the hills, he walked ever
downward to the valley miles
below.

Down, down, down—until the
vegetation thickened into
shrubs, and the desert gave

way to river jungles.

And there where water lapped
at his fatigue, he heard a
singer, singing his compelling
carols to the empty air.

The tradesman knew that it was just
an earth song, for it was
different from the Star-Song
which begged him be its singer—
yet somehow like it.

The River Singer finished and
they walked into the trees.

"Are you the Troubadour, who
knows the Ancient Star-Song?"
the tradesman softly asked.

"No, *you* are the Great Troubadour
for whom the songless world,
so long has waited," the
River Singer said. "Sing, for many
years now, I have hungered
to hear the Ancient Star-Song . . ."

"I am a tradesman only . . ."

Then the River Singer waded out
into the water and beckoned
with his hand. Slowly
the tradesman followed.

They stopped waist-deep in
water. Their eyes swam and
they waited for the music
to begin.

It did.

The tradesman knew the River
Singer heard it too.

The water swirled around them
and the music surged.

Every chord seemed to fuse the
world in oneness.

They stood until the surging
current buried them in song.
It then receded and the music
died away.

And the river was once more a
simple river.

Then over that thin silver
stream the thunder pealed, and
a voice called from the sky
above...

"Tradesman! You are
the Troubadour! Go
now and sing!"

IV

I knew a blind man
whom a surgeon
helped to see. The
doctor never had a
lover such as he.
It is in such a way
that singers love
composers.

From the river, he moved on
and on in quietness alone.

He still talked to Earthmaker
as he always had but now he
called him "Father-Spirit."
He loved the newer name.

The Star-Song came upon him
with a manly joy.

At last he sang!

He threw the song against the
basalt canyon walls.

It ricocheted in splendor,
and he remembered far before
that he had sung those very
canyons into being.

"Father-Spirit!" he shouted
at the desert sky, "I love you.
Ask of me anything you will
and I will do it all."

The universe gathered up the
echoes of his joy and answered
back, "I love you, too, my
Singer. One thing alone I ask
of you:

Sing my Ancient Star-
Song to the world."

"Father-Spirit, I will sing it,
in every country will I sing

it, till all the world you love
can sing it."

In joy he sang and sang until
he fell asleep upon the desert
floor.

V

Hate sometimes
stands quite
close to love.

God too stands
often near to
evil—like si-
lent chessmen—
side by side.
Only the color
of the squares
is different.

He was not alone when he awoke.

The ancient World Hater had
come upon his resting place
and not by chance.

The Hater leered at him with
one defiant, impish grin.

"Hello, Singer!"

"Hello, World Hater," the
Troubadour responded.

"You know my name, old friend
of man?"

"As you know mine, old enemy of
God."

"What brings you to the desert?"

"The Giver of the Song!"

"And does he let you sing it
only in these isolated spots?"

"I only practice here to sing it
in the crowded ways!"

It was hard to sing before the
World Hater, for he ground each
joyous stanza underneath his heel.

The music only seemed to make
the venom in his hate more
bitter than before.

The Hater drew a silver flute
from underneath his studded
belt. He placed it to his
leathered lips drawn tight to
play a melody.

The song surprisingly was
sweet. It filled the canyon
with an airy-tune and hung its
lingering reverberations myster-
iously in every cleft. It
rippled on the very ground
around their feet.

A strange compulsion came upon
the Singer. Furiously he wanted
so to sing the Hater's tune.

He barely staunched the eager
urge to sing.

The morning sun glinted fire
upon the silver flute. The music
and the dazzling light appeared
to mesmerize the Singer.

"You must not sing the Hater's
song," the Father-Spirit cried,
"Be very careful, for I love you,
Troubadour."

"Now," cried the World Hater,
"Let's do this tune at once.
I'll pipe, you sing. Think of
the thousand kingdoms that will
dance about our feet."

"No, Hater, I'll not sing your melodies,"
the Troubadour replied.

"What then Singer will you sing?"

"The Ancient Star-Song of the
Father-Spirit."

"Alone, without accompaniment?"

"Yes, Hater, all alone if need be."

"You need my pipe, man."

"You need my song instead."

"The music of your song is far
beyond my tiny pipe."

"Then, go! For I shall never sing
a lesser piece."

Then all at once the Troubadour
began again. The mountains
amplified his song. It swirled
as sunlit symphony, until
the Hater put his pipe beneath
his belt and fled before
the song of love.

"Beloved Singer, beware the
World Hater," the Father-Spirit said.

Then upward there the Singer
stretched his arms and said
again, "I love you, Father-Spirit."

He waited there a moment while
the sky embraced him and then
he walked away. Ahead he saw
the cities rise, and people
thronged the crowded ways.

VI

If she has loved
him, a man will
carry anything
for his mother—
a waterpot or a
world.

Where first to sing?" he thought.

He turned back to the highlands where he had left the broken tool so useless on the vise.

For days he walked. The dust flew up around his feet as he walked home.

At length, he passed the village signpost and there by odd coincidence, his mother at that very time stood by the well.

They met.

He reached to carry her stone jar.

"It's not traditional," she said.

He took it anyway.

Her cares had made her fifty years seem even more.

"You broke your hammer on the vise," she said. "I had it mended for you."

"I'm through with hammers, anyway," he said. "I've just come home to board the shop."

"And then you'll leave?"

"I will," he said.

"Where will you go?" She
studied paving stones as on they
walked. He moved the heavy jar
to ride upon his other shoulder.

"Wherever there are crowds of
many people."

"The Great Walled City of the
Ancient King?"

"Yes, I suppose."

He feared to talk to her. Yet
he must tell her of the River
Singer and all about the Star-
Song, he had so lately sung.
He seemed afraid that she would
think him mad. He could not
bear to hurt her. For besides
the Father-Spirit, he loved her
most of all. At length he knew
he must lay bare his heart.

"You seem so troubled, son," she
said.

"Not for myself," he said. Then
with the hand that was not needed
in balancing the jar, he took
her hand and smiled.

"I hate for you to board the
shop and leave..."

"Am I the tradesman that my father

was, while still he was alive?"
he asked.

"You both were good, but somehow
wood is never kind to your great
hands. Your father's hands never
paid the pain it cost you, just
to love his trade."

She looked down at the gentle,
suffering hand that held her own.
Somewhere in her swimming recol-
lection, she remembered the
same hand with infant fingers
that had clutched the ringlets of her
hair and reached to feel the
leathered face of Eastern Kings.
But he could not remember that.

They walked still further without
speaking.

"MOTHER, I AM THE SINGER!" He
blurted out at once.

"I know," she said.

"I love the Father-Spirit more
than life. He has sent me to
the crowded ways to sing the
Ancient Star-Song."

"I know," she said again. "I
heard the Ancient Star-Song
only once. It was the very
night that you were born. And
all these years, my son, I've
known that you would come to
board the shop someday. Can
you sing the Star-Song yet?"

"I can," he answered back.

They neared a house and entered.
They shared a simple meal
and sat in silence. And the song,
which they alone of all the world
did know, was lingering all
around them in the air.

She had not heard its strains
for thirty years but hungered for
its music.

He had not sung it for an after-
noon but longed to have its
fluid meaning coursing through
his soul.

Of course the song began.

VII

Before the song all
music came like
muted, empty octaves
begging a composer's pen.
The notes cried silently
for paper staves and
kept their sound in theory only.

In the beginning was
　　the song of love.
Alone in empty nothingness
　　and space
It sang itself through
　　vaulted halls above
Reached gently out to
　　touch the Father's face.

And all the tracklessness
　　where worlds would be
Cried "Father" through the
　　aching void. Sound tore
The distant chasm, and eternity
Called back—"I love you Son—
　　sing Troubadour."

His melody fell upward
　　into joy
And climbed its way
　　in spangled rhapsody.
Earthmaker's infant stars
　　adored his boy,
And blazed his name through
　　every galaxy.

"Love," sang the Spirit Son
　　and mountains came.
More melody, and life
　　began to grow.
He sang of light, and darkness
　　fled in shame
Before a universe in
　　embryo.

Then on the naked ground
　　the Troubadour

Knelt down and firmly sang
   a stronger chord.
He scooped the earth dust
   in his hand
And worked the clay
   till he had molded man.

They laid him down beneath
   primeval trees
And waited there. They loved
   him while he slept
And both rejoiced as he began
   to breathe
A triumph etched in brutal
   nakedness.

"I am a Man!" the sun-crowned
   being sang.
He stood and brushed away the
   clinging sand.
He knew from where his very
   being sprang.
Wet clay still dripped from
   off the Singer's hands.

Earthmaker viewed the sculptured
   dignity
Of man, God-like and strident,
   President
Of everything that was,
   content to be
God's intimate and only earthen
   friend.

The three embraced in that
   primeval glen.
And then God walked away,
   his Singer too.
Hate came—discord—they
   never met again.

The new man aged and died
and dying grew
A race of doubtful, death-owned
sickly men.
And every child received the
planet's scar
And wept for love to come and
reign. And then
To heal hate-sickened life
both wide and far.

"We're naked!" cried the
new men in their shame.
(they really were)
A race of piteous things
who had no name.

They died absurdly whimpering
for life.
They probed their sin for
rationality.
Self murdered self in endless
hopeless strife
And holiness slept with
indecency.

All birth was but the prelude
unto death
And every cradle swung above
a grave.
The sun made weary trips from
east to west,
Time found no shore, and
culture screamed and raved.

The world, in peaceless orbits,
sped along
And waited for the Singer and
his song.

VIII

It is always much more
difficult to sing when
the audience has turned
its back.

The Singer ceased.

The Ancient Star-Song slept.

"You know the final verse?"
his mother asked.

"I know it all," he answered
back. "But I'll not sing it
here. I'll wait till I am on
the wall. Then alone the
melody will fall upon thick
ears."

"They will not like the final
verse," she said.

"They will not like it, for its
music is beyond their empty days
and makes them trade their
littleness for life."

"The self of every singer of the
song must die to know its music?"

"They all must die, and ever
does the self die hard. It
screams and begs in pity not to
go. Nor can it bear to let the
Father-Spirit own the soul."

He turned the thoughts methodi-
cally within his mind then spoke
again, "Mother, I shall sing the
song while I move out to seek
more singers who like me are
quite content to sing, then die."

She knew that he was right, but
found it hard to talk of joyous
life and painful death at the
same time. How odd the song born
on Earthmaker's breath should
lead his only Troubadour to death.

"I cannot bear to see you
    die. Let all
The world go by. Don't
    sing upon the wall.
At least don't sing the
    hell-bound ancient curse.
If you must sing of life
    leave off the final verse."

"I go," he said. "God give me
strength to sing upon the wall—
the Great Walled City of the
Ancient King."

He turned.

She cried.

"Leave off the final verse and
not upon the wall."

He kissed her.

"I can't ignore
    the Father-Spirit's call
So I will sing it there,
    and I will sing it all."

IX

A healthy child is
somehow very much
like God. A hurting
child, his son.

The sunlight lured him from the shaded, village streets and drew him into day. And everywhere he went, the World Hater had already been. The sick men lay among the roadside thorns. The old ones groaned from habit. The young ones whimpered out of hopelessness.

The Singer stopped. Beside the road he saw a brown-eyed child. Her mouth was drawn in hard, firm lines that could not bend to either smile or frown. Her sickness ate her spirit, devouring all the sparkle in her eyes.

Her legs misshapen as they were, lay useless underneath the coarsest sort of cloth. The Singer knelt beside her in the dust and touched her limpid hand and cried. He drew the cloth away that hid her legs. He reached his calloused hand and touched the small, misshapen foot.

"I too was born with scarred feet. See mine!" he said, drawing back the hem of his own robe.

She seemed about to speak, when the music of a silver pipe broke in the air around them. He had heard the pipe before.

Above them towered the World
Hater.

"I knew you'd come," he said.
"You will, of course, make
straight her twisted limbs?"

"I will, World Hater... but can
you have no mercy? She's but a
child. Can her wholeness menace
you in any way? Would it so
embarrass you to see her skipping
in the sun? Why hate such
little, suffering life?"

"Why chide me, Singer? She's
Earthmaker's awful error. Tell
your Father-Spirit he should
take more time when he creates."

"No, it is love which brings a
thousand children into life in
health. It is hate that cripples
each exception to eternal joy.
But why must you forever toy
with nature to make yourself
such ugly pastimes of delight?"

"I hate all the Father-Spirit
loves. If he would only hate
the world with me, I'd find no
joy in it again. You sing.
The only music that I know is
the cacophony of agony that
grows from roadside wretches
such as these."

The child between them lay
bewildered by their conversation.
The Singer spoke again:

"I'll bring my song against
    your hate
Against the bonds of human
    sins.
And human tears will all subside
When the Ancient Star-Song wins."

The Hater raged and screamed
above his crippled joy:

"Sing health! If you must.
Sing everybody's but your own.
I soon will have your song,
likewise your life.
Your great Star-Song is
    doomed to fall.
You'll groan my kind
    of music
When I meet you at
    the wall."

The Singer scooped the frightened
child into his arms. He
sang and set her in the sunny
fields and thrilled to watch her
run. The world was hers in a
way she'd never known. The
butterfly-filled meadows danced
her eyes alive and drew her
scurrying away.

And others came!

Untouchables with bandages
heard the healing song and came
to health:

The crippled and the blind.
Sick of soul
Sick of heart

Sick of hate
Sick of mind.
Everywhere the music went, full health
came.

And all the way, men everywhere
were whispering that the long-
awaited Troubadour had come.

"It is he," they said, "at last
he's come. Praise the Father-
Spirit, he has come."

X

The word *crying*
does not appear
in the lexicon
of heaven. It
is the only word
listed in the
lexicon of hell.

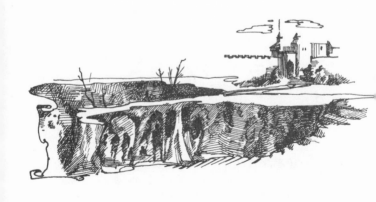

The Singer woke at midnight. In the stupor of half-consciousness—neither quite aware nor yet asleep—he was alone.

The air was full of moans. With groans of grief and pity, the night was crying. He had never heard the darkness cry before.

"Where are you, World Hater?" he shouted.

"Standing in the doorway of the worlds—reveling in my melodies of ugliness and death."

The Singer listened. The morbid air depressed him and he could not help but weep himself. He ached from the despair. "How long have they cried beyond the doorway of the worlds?" he asked.

The World Hater seemed to summon up the volume of their moaning and then he shouted, "They've moaned a million years—
It never stops. They hurt with pain that burns and eats the conscience—illuminating every failure. They never can be free. Crying is the only thing they know."

"Poor souls! Have they nothing

to look back upon with joy?"
the Singer asked.

"No. Nor anything to look forward
to with hope."

"Could they never give up suffering
for one small moment, every
thousand years or so?"

"No. Never. They ache in simply
knowing they will never cease to
ache."

"I'm coming to the Canyon of the
Damned you know."

"You dare not think that you could
sing above their anguished dying
that never will be dead."

"You'll see, World Hater. I will
come."

"It's my domain!" the Hater pro-
tested.

"You have no domain. How dare
you think that you can hold some
corner of Earthmaker's universe
and make it your own private
horror chamber!"

"It is forever, Singer!"

"Yes, but not off-limits to the
song. I'll smash the gates that
hold the damned and every chain
will fall away.

"I'll sing to every suffering
cell of hate, the love song of
my soul.

"I'll stand upon the torment of
the Canyon of the Damned."

The troubled air grew still. The
World Hater stepped outside the
universe—pulled shut the doorway
of the worlds.

And Crying softly slept with Joy.

XI

Oftentimes Love is
so poorly packaged
that when we have
sold everything to
buy it, we cry in
finding all our
substance gone and
nothing in the tin-
sel and the ribbon.

Hate dresses well
to please a buyer.

He met a woman in the street.
She leaned against an open
door and sang through her half-
parted lips a song that he could
barely hear. He knew her friend-
ship was for hire. She was with-
out a doubt a study in desire.
Her hair fell free around her
shoulders. And intrigue played
upon her lips.

"Are you betrothed?" she asked.

"No, only loved," he answered.

"And do you pay for love?"

"No, but I owe it everything."

"You are alone. Could I sell you
but an hour of friendship?"

Deaf to her surface proposition,
he said, "Tell me of the song that
you were singing as I came upon
you. Where did you learn it?"

His question troubled her.
At length she said, "The first
night that I ever sold myself,
I learned it from a tall
impressive man."

"And did he play a silver pipe?"
the Singer asked.

She seemed surprised. "Do you

know the man who bought me
first?"

"Yes. Not long ago, in fact, he
did his best to teach that song
to me."

"I cannot understand. I sell
friendship and you your melody.
Why would he teach us both the
self-same song?"

The Singer pitied her. He knew
the World Hater had a way of making
every victim feel as though
he were the only person who
could sing his song.

"He only has one song; he there-
fore teaches it to everyone. It
is a song of hate."

"No, it is a love song. The first
night that he held me close, he
sang it tenderly and so in every
way he owned me while he sang
to me of love."

"And have you seen him since?"

"No, not him, but a never ending
queue of men with his desires."

"So it was no song of love. Tell
me, did he also say that some
day in the merchandising of your
soul, you would find someone who
would not simply leave his fee
upon the stand but rather take
you home to care for you and

cherish you?"

Again she seemed surprised, "Those
were indeed his very words—how
can you know them?"

"And have you found the one that
he has promised?"

"Not yet."

"And how long have you peddled
friendship?"

"Some twenty years are gone since
first I learned the song that you
inquired about."

The Singer felt a burst of pity.
"We sometimes give ourselves
to hate in masquerade and only
think it love. And all our lives
we sing the song we thought
was right. The Canyon of the Damned
is filled with singers who
thought they knew a love song...
Listen while I sing for you
a song of love."

He began the melody so vital
to the dying men around him.
"In the beginning was the song of
love..."

She listened and knew for the
first time she was hearing all of
love there was. Her eyes swam
when he was finished. She sobbed
and sobbed in shame. "Forgive me,
Father-Spirit, for I am sinful

and undone . . . for singing weary
years of all the wrong words . . ."

The Singer touched her shoulder
and told her of the joy that lay
ahead if she could learn the
music he had sung.

He left her in the street and
walked away, and as he left he
heard her singing his new song.
And when he turned to wave the
final time he saw her shaking
her head to a friendship buyer.
She would not take his money.

And from his little distance,
the Singer heard her use his
very words.

"Are you betrothed?" the buyer
asked her.

"No, only loved," she answered.

"And do you pay for love?"

"No, but I owe it everything."

XII

In hell there is no music—
an agonizing night that
never ends as songless as
a shattered violin.

S ing the Hillside Song!" they cried.

There were so many of them. He wasn't even sure he could be heard above the din of all their voices. He walked among them and looked them over. In his mind he knew that the Father-Spirit wanted each of them to learn his song.

Someone in the sprawling crowd stood and handed him a lyre. "Sing for us please Singer—the Hillside Song!"

"Yes, yes," they called, "the Hillside Song."

He looked down at the lyre and held it close. He turned each thumbset till the string knew how to sound, then he began:

"Blessed are the musical," he said, "for theirs shall be a never-ending song."

"Blessed are those who know the difference between their loving and their lusting, for they shall be pure in heart and understand the reason."

"Blessed are those who die for reasons that are real, for they themselves are real."

"Blessed are all those who yet
can sing when all the theater
is empty and the orchestra is gone."

"Blessed is the man who stands
before the cruelest king and
only fears his God."

"Blessed is the mighty king who
sits beside the weakest man and
thinks of all their similarities."

"Earthmaker is love. He has sent
his only Troubadour to close
the Canyon of the Damned."

Then they broke his song and cried
out with one voice, "Tell us
Singer, have you any hope for us?
Can we be saved?"

"You may if you will sing Earth-
maker's Song!"

"Is there another way to cheat
the Canyon of the Damned?"

"None but the Song!"

XIII

No person ever is so helpless as
the man in whom joy and misery
sleep comfortably together.

No physician can give health and
happiness to the man who enjoys
his affliction. For such a man
health and happiness are always
contradictory.

From night to day and back to
night again he travelled on.
He saw the glow of the great city,
far on the horizon, and just
the light of it roused expectancy
and fear. By twilight he was
weary and he turned aside to
sleep beside a moonlit stream.
The water fell in froth and white
cascades into the wooden lattice
of a creaking wheel.

The Miller who was still at work
seemed most determined to finish
out his toil by starlight. It
was only by the merest chance he
found the Singer sleeping by the
stream just above the giant wheel.

For a moment he saw the Singer only
as a vagrant and was inclined to
drive him from the premises. But
then he changed his mind and
invited him to share the evening
meal.

As they went into the grain room,
the Singer looked upon the great
machine which turned the giant
stones which milled the grist.

The Singer was about to ask him
where he found the mason to
quarry such impressive stones,
when suddenly he discovered that
one of the Miller's hands was
badly scarred and crippled.

"Can you run so great a stone
with but a single hand?" The
Singer asked.

"I manage . . . though it always was
much easier with two."

"Did you lose your hand in this
machinery?"

"I was in much too great a hurry
three harvest-times ago. I was
trying to sweep the grist away
when I dropped my broom upon the
floor stone. When I reached to
pick it up, the great stone caught
my arm and hand. And when they
rolled the grinder back, this was
all that I had left," he said.

"I will," observed the Singer,
"make it useful once again if you
will just desire it whole and
believe it can be."

"It cannot be so easy, Singer.
Would you wave your magic wand
above such suffering and have it
all be done with? I sometimes
wake at midnight with a searing
flame of fire and throbbing
agony alive through all this
twisted, dying limb. You have
both hands and cannot understand
this sort of pain."

"I have no pain like yours, but
I have a healing melody. Earth-
maker gave the song to me for
healing hands like yours.

Already it has helped a little
girl to be made whole.''

''Was her hand as badly mangled
as my own?''

''It was her legs—but yes, they
were...''

''How often I have wished that I
might trade a useless hand for such
a leg,'' the Miller interrupted.

''Why either—why not simply be
made whole?''

''Oh that such a healing now were
possible—the speed I might regain
in working at the mill. But no, it
cannot be. Can you not under-
stand? Have you no sympathy
for suffering? Are you so
empty of conscience as to suggest
a hopeless remedy. You only add
to misery by forcing me to see
myself a cripple. I soon shall
have to close the mill or sell it.
I cannot make the necessary
quota since the accident occurred.''

''There is power within the Melody
I know to make you well. Please,
Miller, trust and let me sing and
you will run the mill alone
with two good hands.''

''Stop your mocking. I am a
sick old man whom life has cheated
of a hand. The nightly pain has
already now begun. The season

of my hope is gone."

The Singer watched him caught in
some dread spasm of his aching cir-
cumstance. He moaned and fell
upon the floor and with his healthy
fingers he held his mangled hand.

His surging pain caused him to
cry, "O God deliver me from this
body . . . I never can be well
and whole as other men."

He waited for the Singer to join
him in his pity, but when he
raised his head for understanding,
the door stood open on the night
and the Singer was nowhere to
be seen.

XIV

To God obscenity is not uncovered
flesh. It is exposed intention.
Nakedness is just a state of heart.
Was Adam any more unclothed when
he discovered shame? Yes.

The wall of the great city reached
upward till it defied all measurement
of mind.

Outside the fortress, stretching
up the slopes, a grove of trees
bearded the great stone wall that
had slept for centuries above the seasons
of new leaf and naked frost.

Towers and minarets glinted
in the sun-washed sky and caused
the Singer apprehension as he
leaned against a tree.

He watched the human commerce flow-
ing through the rough-hewn gates.
Never had he seen so many people
hungry for a living song. They
jostled shapelessly, a mass of urban
sameness. Each hurried after
urgent unattended business, yet
none had any reason for the press.

The Singer sighed.

Sometimes a child would follow in
the madding throng. Already it
appeared the youngster tried to
learn the routine, manufactured steps
of older men he mimicked in the way.

Reluctant to adopt the business
cadence of the empty throng,
the Singer turned and sought a quiet
place beneath the wall. He walked
into the trees.

"Hello, Singer," said the voice he
knew too well. "Welcome to the
quiet of the grove. Does the
senseless empty crowd offend you?"

The Singer's only offense came in
knowing that the World Hater always
seemed to know what he was thinking.

"How did you manage to make them
cherish all this nothingness?"
he asked the World Hater.

"I simply make them feel embarrassed
to admit that they are incomplete. A
man would rather close his eyes than
see himself as your Father-Spirit
does. I teach them to exalt their
emptiness and thus preserve the
dignity of man."

"They need the dignity of God."

"You tell them that. I sell a
cheaper product."

They were deeper in the woods.
They stopped in a shaded spot
beneath the fortress wall.

A heavy set of chains hung from
a great foundation stone that
held the towering wall. Manacles
hung bolted on the wrists of a
burly, naked man.

He slept or seemed to.

Before him on the ground lay a
heavy stoneware basin nearly

filled with water and the dried
remains of bread half-eaten.

"Is he mad?" the Singer asked.

"Senselessly," the Hater answered.

"Who brings him bread and water?"

"I do."

"Why?"

"To see him dance in madness
without a tiny hope! Imagine my
delight when he raves and screams
in chains. Would you like for me
to wake this animal?"

"He is a man. Earthmaker made him
so. What is his name?"

"The Crowd."

"Why such a name?"

"Because within this sleeping hulk
there are a thousand hating spirits
from the Canyon of the Damned. They
leap at him with sounds no ears but
his can hear. They dive at him with
screaming lights no other eyes can
see. And in his torment he will
hold his shaggy head and whimper.
Then he rises and strains in fury
against the chains to tear them
from the wall. Stand back and see."

The Hater took the silver pipe out
of its sheath. The tune began—a

choppy, weird progression of half
tones.

The sleeping giant stirred and placed
his massive hands upon his temples.
In fever hot the Hater played and just
as rapidly the Madman stumbled to his
feet.

The Singer never had beheld so
great a man as he. Some unseen,
unheard agony rippled through
his bleeding soul. He growled,
then screamed and tried to tear the
chains that held him to the wall.

"Stop, Hater!" cried the Singer.

But the Hater played more loudly
than before. At that precise and
ugly moment, the pinion on the left
gave way. The chain fell loose.
Then with his one free hand the monster
tore the other chain away. In but
a second he stood unchained
before them. The Hater took his
pipe and fled into the trees. The
Singer then began to sing and
continued on until the Madman stood
directly in his path. With love
that knew no fear, the Singer
caught his torment, wrapped it all
in song and gave it back to him as
peace.

And soon the two men held each other.
In their long embrace of soul, the
spirits cried and left. They
stood at last alone.

"What year is it?" the giant asked
with some perplexity.

"It is the year of the Troubadour,"
the Singer said. "How long have
you hung upon the wall and writhed
in madness?"

"I cannot tell the years."

"Will you come with me into the
ancient city?"

"Yes," said the Madman, and then
remembering, he added, "I cannot,
for I am naked."

"Not if you love me. He whom
Earthmaker loves," replied the
Troubadour, "is hidden from his
shame forevermore."

"I love you more than life," the
Madman then confessed.

And when they turned to leave the
two of them were dressed.

XV

Humanity is fickle.
They may dress for a
morning coronation and
never feel the need to
change clothes to
attend an execution in
the afternoon.

So Triumphal Sundays
and Good Fridays
always fit comfortably
into the same April
week.

The way through the gates was full.
The Holiday had come and the
eagerness of all the citizens for
tradition and festivity had charged
the air with expectation. The
Singer and the Madman felt the strain
of something dread but pending,
threatening but unannounced.

Within the press of people the Singer
felt a mixing of compassion and
revulsion. He pitied them for
emptiness but resented their con-
tentment in it. He knew that what
they needed was the Song.

When they approached the gates, a
woman in the crowd came to the
Madman, then shuddering fell
back in fright. They stopped and
the congestion moved around
them.

"You are the Madman," she said.
Then changing her mind she denied
it, "No you are clothed and sane."

"I am the Madman," he said, "but the
Troubadour has come and I am full
and whole."

"Who is this Troubadour?" she asked.

"He is the Son of Earthmaker!"

A crowd was gathering around
their conversation.

"Listen to me," called the
Madman to the crowd.

"I hung upon the wall until
this very hour. When the moon
was full I roamed in wild
unholy grottoes of my mind. See
these wrists," he said pulling
back his sleeves.

The marks and scars of chafing
steel were obvious to all.

"The manacles of iron did this.
I could kill and would have
many times except for the great
chains which held me. I cried
within the grove and wished to
die. I tore at every band and
tried to set my own brutality
toward freedom, but never did the
chains give way until today."

"Stop!" cried a voice within the
crowd. "You are still mad," the
voice continued as the Hater
came out of the crowd. "Listen
to me, Madman," he said pulling
out the silver pipe.

Beads of perspiration appeared
upon the Madman's brow. Fear
tore at him—could he stand
the melody that formerly had
driven him insane? The weird
progression of shrieking notes
began.

But the Madman's tension soon
began to ease. In the frustration

of his losing, the Hater played
more loudly than before.

Soon the Madman was entirely at
peace. He exulted in the confi-
dence of total sanity. "It's
no use Hater, the Troubadour has
come."

The crowd had grown to several
hundred people and the Madman
called out over them, "This
man's pipe wiped out all my
sanity until today. I learned a
new song from the Singer for whom
the world so long has waited.
Listen to the Song of Life."

He began to sing. The Singer
himself was startled at the beauty
of his voice. He sang with such
confidence that none could doubt
the meaning he found springing up
within his soul.

"Where did you learn this confi-
dence and joy?" they asked him.

He nodded toward the Singer.
"He has saved me from myself
and from a thousand maddened spirits
from the Canyon of the Damned."

"Who are you, Man?" they asked the
Singer.

"I am the Troubadour, the Son of
Earthmaker," the Singer then
replied. "I have come
to save the world and close

the Canyon of the Damned."

"Can we know your saving song
and sing it as the Madman does?"

"You may, if you believe I
am the only Troubadour."

They mulled the proposition
in their muddled minds.

Then someone in the fringe cried
loudly, "Halana to the Troubadour,
Son of Earthmaker!" Another to the
far left took up the cry. A third
and then a fourth—and suddenly
the world seemed caught up in the
cry.

"Halana to the Troubadour,
Earthmaker's only Son."

Through the ancient city gates the joy
echoed down the plaster canyons and
drubbed its cadence over cobblestones.
The cry became a tumult in the city,
    Joy to the Earth,
    The Troubadour has come
    Make ready for the Song of Life.

A thousand dancers swelled the streets
and instruments of music gathered up
the merriment of holiday. Every
street cried out the newness of the
singing age that came to close
the joyless era that had gone before.

The music swept through every city street
and purged the evil and the sin
before it. The Hater dropped his

pipe and barely could retrieve it
from beneath the thousand driving feet.

The Song had come, and for one
swelling surge of love there was
no room for hate.

Even the sentinels upon the
walls raised their hands, threw their
bearded faces to the sky and cried
out over all the world beneath them,
"Halana to the Troubadour,
Earthmaker's only Son."

XVI

SYLLOGISM

Major Premise:
God is a custom.

Minor Premise:
A custom is an
old, old habit.

Conclusion:
Therefore, God is
an old, old habit.

The singing and the dancing swept
the crowd in joyful madness till
all the city gathered in the
Plaza of Humanity—a colonnaded
forum around the Shrine of Older Life.

The Shrine of Older Life was
attended by the Keepers of the
Ancient Ways. They were every
one gray-bearded and wore the
pointed hats, the custom of their
ordered service at the shrine.
Each sang the hymns of their
tradition and kept with strict
obedience the rituals of the ages.

Since the Holiday of Hope had come
the Grand Musician was himself the
chief director of the liturgy.
The formality of the great high
adoration was broken by the singing
and dancing crowd that swept
through the Holy Square. The Singer
went before them in a sea of warm
approval till he stood beneath the
towering Shrine of Older Life. It
glittered in the sun and lifted up its
marble proclamation to the world.

An acolyte of lower caste rang a
brazen gong that brought the
roaring crowd to silence and only
then did the Grand Musician rise
to speak.

"What does this uproar mean?" he
asked.

A single voice rose from the sea
of faces. "We have found the long-
awaited Troubadour. He knows the
Ancient Star-Song!"

"Yes! Yes!" cried the throng, "He
knows the Ancient Star-Song—He is
the Troubadour, Son of Earthmaker!"
The mere suggestion of the joyous
prose began the cries of "Halana"
all over again. Once again the
gong restored a silence to the square.
The Grand Musician turned to the Singer.

"Is it true? Are you the Troubadour?
Can you sing the Ancient Star-Song?"

"I am he. I know the song."

"Then sing it now," agreed the Keep-
ers of the Ancient Ways.

The Singer took his lyre and strummed
the strings. The chords fell
outward over all the throng.

The audience grew still. He sang
the very words he first had sung
before his mother. Above him towered
the wall and high upon the bulwark
he saw the framework of a strange machine.
It was the great machine on which
false singers met their death.

He knew then what it meant to sing
a new song.

And then his finger swept the strings
and he began the final verse.

XVII

A finale is not always the best
song but it is always the last.

The Father and his Troubadour
  sat down
Upon the outer rim of space.
  "And here,
My Singer," said Earthmaker,
  "is the crown
Of all my endless skies—the
  green, brown sphere
Of all my hopes." He reached
  and took the round
New planet down, and held it
  to his ear.

"They're crying, Troubadour,"
  he said. "They cry
So hopelessly." He gave the
  little ball
Unto his Son, who also held
  it by
His ear. "Year after weary
  year they all
Keep crying. They seem born to
  weep then die.
Our new man taught them crying
  in the Fall.

"It is a peaceless globe.
  Some are sincere
In desperate desire to see
  her freed
Of her absurdity. But
  war is here.
Men die in conflict, bathed
  in blood and greed."

Then with his nail he scraped
   the atmosphere
And both of them beheld the
   planet bleed.

Earthmaker set earth spinning
   on its way
And said, "Give me your vast
   infinity
My son; I'll wrap it in a bit
   of clay.
Then enter Terra microscop-
   ically
To love the little souls who
   weep away
Their lives." "I will," I said,
   "set Terra free."

And then I fell asleep and all
   awareness fled.
I felt my very being shrinking
   down.
My vastness ebbed away. In dwind-
   ling dread,
All size decayed. The universe
   around
Drew back. I woke upon a tiny
   bed
Of straw in one of Terra's
   smaller towns.

And now the great reduction
   has begun:
Earthmaker and his Troubadour
   are one.
And here's the new redeeming
   melody—
The only song that can set
   Terra free.

The Shrine of older days
  must be laid by.
Mankind must see Earthmaker
  left the sky,
And he is with us. They must
  concede that
I am he. They must believe the
  Song or die.

XVIII

Vengeance *(ven'jəns) noun*
1. Eye for eye, tooth for tooth;
a fair, satisfying and rapid
way to a sightless, toothless
world.

Mercy *(mer'sē) noun*
1. The infrequent art of turning
thumbs up on an old antagonist
at the end of one's rapier.

Liar," cried the Keepers of the Ancient Ways, when he had finished with his song. "We've kept this Shrine for many years as our fathers did before us. Earthmaker loves the shrine he gave us. He will meet us here forever."

"No," cried the Singer. "Please believe the Song. Earthmaker never will again meet men within this holy square."

"Liar!" they cried again. "Strike him on the mouth." A bearded monk, who only lately read the liturgy, laid aside his scroll and struck the Singer on the mouth. The blood ran down his chin.

"Listen, men of Terra!" cried the Grand Musician. "He sings a lie. Earthmaker loves the Shrine. He has loved it for a thousand holidays."

The Singer stumbled to his feet and cried above the crowd. "Earthmaker loves neither shrines nor holidays. He loves only men. Life is the Song and not the Shrine." Another Keeper of the Ancient Ways laid aside his incense and his holy book and struck him in the face. He fell once more.

The Madman who had lately sung in joy the great Halana Chorus was

bewildered by this furious turn of
circumstance. When they struck
the Singer the second time he rushed
upon the Keepers of the Ancient Ways.
He attacked them with such fury that
they fell away in fright. Then
suddenly a sentinel struck him from
behind and sent him sprawling in
the dust unconscious. In a moment
they had him clamped securely in the
irons.

"Listen," cried a voice above the
tumult of the moment. The Singer
knew the voice. It was the World
Hater masquerading as a Keeper of
the Ancient Ways. He wore the mask
of those who led in worship at the
Shrine.

"Listen," he said again, "this man
in irons is mad. For years he hung
in chains and quite away from all
that he might hurt until today.
The Singer freed him to attack and
hoped that he might injure the Keepers
of the Ancient Ways.

"Look at him," said the masquerading
World Hater, pointing to the
Singer. "Does he appear a Holy
Singer? Where are his prayer book
and candle? If he had come to
worship, would he not have brought
along a scroll of ancient truths?
If his song is from the Father-
Spirit, why did it not come to us
through the Grand Musician? He
wears no robe, he has no beard
like other holy men. Where is his

pointed hat? He was but a tradesman
in the northern hills. He
never studied music like the Grand
Musician. Is it reasonable to
suppose that God would give a tradesman
a song that he withheld from those
who keep his very Shrine?"

The Grand Musician rose and sang.
Infirmly at the first, but gaining
confidence, he sang the Anthem of
the great Shrine.

"Blessed be Thou, O Earthmaker,
Lover of the ancient days
May we adore the ancient truths,
Walk only on the ancient ways."

Gradually the crowd began to join
the Grand Musician.

"Keep Thy Shrine a sacred place
For practice of Thy timeless lore
Of ancient holy men who taught us
Great traditions we adore."

Finally from the habit of their
worship all the crowd rose up to
sing the songless melody they had
learned from the generations who
had left them with the weariness
of worship.

"Blessed art Thou, O Earthmaker,
Help of ours in ages past,
Keep Thy holy Shrine forever,
Never changing truth Thou hast."

"Long live Earthmaker!" cried a
gray-beard Keeper of the Ancient

Ways. "Long live Earthmaker," he
repeated. "Long live the Shrine of
Older Life."

And all of them called out together,
"Long live Earthmaker. Long live
the Shrine of Older Life."

"What shall we do, O Grand Musician,
with the Liar who hates the Shrine
of Older Life?" cried the Hater
still in masquerade.

"We shall smash his lyre and . . ."
Before he could name the sentence,
a small bent man made his way to
the steps of the Shrine. It was
the Miller with the injured hand.
"May I speak before you pass the
sentence?" the Miller asked the
Grand Musician.

"You may," he answered back.

"I am a miller. My home is by the
grainfields of the east. Three
years ago my hand was crushed in
an accident at my own mill. This
liar who calls himself the only
Troubadour mocked my crushed
deformity and left me screaming in
the night."

"Had you no pity, Singer,
for this man?" the Grand Musician
asked.

"He had pity enough for himself.
I could have made him whole," the
Singer said.

"How can you call yourself Earth-
maker's Son and have no pity?
Earthmaker is merciful and filled
with love." He paced the marble
stones before the crowd. At
length he spoke, "Because you
had no pity your hand shall be
like his."

He thought once more and said,
"And now I pass the sentence. We
shall break his lyre, then we shall
break his hand and set him free.
On the flesh of his forehead we
shall burn the word 'Liar' and he
shall live beneath his sentence
all his life. So shall the sentence
be of anyone who claims to be
Earthmaker's Son and sings a song
which desecrates the Shrine.

"Bring out the block and mallet."

The guards obeyed. They placed the
Singer's hand upon the block and
brought the crushing mallet down.

The Singer winced.

The Miller walked up to the Singer
who gently held his injured hand.

"Would you like pity from me,
Singer?" he said through his teeth.
"Here, Singer, is the only kind of
pity that you know." He spit into
the Singer's face and laughed.

The Madman strained against the
chains and was about to rip them

free. His struggle ended in futility.
He could not look upon the
suffering of the only man who knew
him sane. He cried to see the
spit of hate coursing down the
Singer's face.

"Crush his other hand before you set
him free," cried someone in the
crowd. "Teach him through great pain
that Earthmaker pities injury."

"It's true he must learn how to care,"
the Grand Musician cried. "Place his
other hand upon the block."

Once more the mallet fell and the
splintering of tendons shot burning
agony throughout the Singer's soul.

They laid his lyre upon the block
and smashed it with the mallet
that had fallen twice before.

"Sing for us!" they cried in vengeance.
"Play and sing!" they said.

The Grand Musician turned his head
and sang an ancient hymn while they
spit again upon the Singer and
struck him with their fists.

"You were going to heal the Miller's
hand," cried someone in the crowd.
"Sing healing to your own."

When the Grand Musician finished singing
all the ancient hymn, he turned
back to the Singer who gazed in agony
upon his broken hands. "Bring the

fire and irons and we shall etch the
name upon his face."

They seared the word across his
forehead ... L I A R.

The Madman held his shaggy face and
cried into his hands. His sobbing
went unnoticed in the action of
the trial.

"May I now release this false
Troubadour?" the Grand Musician
asked.

"No. He must die upon the wall.
Let him suffer for his lies. Let
him hang where everyone may know
the nature of his ugly melodies of
desecration. Hang him on the
great machine of death."

"Yes! Yes!" they cried in fevered
chanting. "Yes! Yes! thou Great
Musician! Yes! Hang him on the
great machine of death."

XIX

Institutions have a poor safety record. The guillotines of orthodoxy keep a clean blade that is always honed for heresy. And somewhere near the place where witches die an unseen sign is posted whose invisible letters clearly read:
WE ARE PROUD TO REPORT
0 WORKING DAYS LOST TO
INJURY OR ACCIDENT.
—THE MANAGEMENT

Let us pray.

The sentinels returned the Madman
to the grove. He followed them
without a struggle. He walked
along in the stupefaction of his
disbelief. In his former
madness he would have crushed the
wardens in the foment of his rage.
He could scarcely understand that
in a single day he had been
granted both a new mind and an
injured heart.

The day's proceedings had been too
much for him. Every time he closed
his eyes, he saw the mallet of the
executioner again: The splintering
of tendons, the wincing of the Singer,
the facial blows the priest had
given him: all these made his mind
a horror chamber.

Somewhere in his reverie of agony
they reached the wall. The attendants
locked him in the irons, while
he stared vacantly away. They
brought him bread and water, which
he never saw.

He only wept. A tremor shook his
giant frame.

The darkness came. The Madman cried.
While somewhere higher on the wall
the Singer died.

It was good the Madman could not
behold his suffering. He could

not have borne it. A trinity of
other lovers came, all three
absorbed in one great hurt.
The little girl sat down between
the older women.

"I am his mother," said the oldest.
"I am the demonstration of his
power," said the little girl.
"I am only a friend," said the
other woman.

"I gave him life," said his mother.
"I gave him twisted feet," said the
little girl.
"I gave him shame," said the friend.

"He taught me obedience to the Father-
Spirit," said the mother.
"He taught me running."
"He taught me love."

They sat beneath the great machine of
death. It was a trebled pietà of
stone and still it wept.

"I feel very old today," said the
mother as she placed her arm around
the shoulder of the little girl.

"I feel as though I soon must
watch the Father-Spirit die." The
girl sobbed into the bosom of the
Singer's mother.

The Friendship Seller was a
world away. She said, "I am
ashamed of being human. It
is the very shame I felt the first
time that I . . ." She could not

bring herself to tell her ugly
fall before the grieving child.
"The moment that I saw the Keeper
of the Ancient Ways who was chief
accuser, I knew he bore some vague
familiarity. He was no priest..."

"I know," the older woman said.

"He was the piper who taught me a
song of death and called it love,"
the Friendship Seller said.

"I knew him too," said the little
girl. "He used to pass me where
I begged, and look upon my twisted
legs and laugh. I used to feel so
bad when he would look and smirk
in satisfaction. And every time he
passed he left me crying."

They ceased their talking and
looked up at the wall. The great
machine hung heaviness into
their souls, the giant timbers
creaked in the ordeal they were
asked to undergo. The women shuddered
when they viewed the suffering
form that lay among the cables
and the gears.

Grief owned the day.

In turn the three stood up and
stared upon the dying Singer, high
and lifted up.

"My joy, my health," said the little
girl.

"My life," said the Friendship Seller.

The night stood dumb. The burdened
mother wept. "The Ancient Star-
Song lost. The World Hater won.
I wish I might have died instead
of you, my son, my son, my son."

XX

A child who cries at the
coffin of his father is
only mature when he has
lived long enough to cry
at the coffin of his son.

Never was a boy crucified,
but that the weeping Father
always found the nail-prints
in his own hands.

The dying went slowly. The great
timbers were weathered by
the grimness of their task. A
single, great gear pivoted upon
an axis, that culminated in a
windlass upon which wound a cable.
Below in an ever tightening arc an
armature was turning. A group of
smaller cams and gears seemed each
to play their part in keeping
tension on the heavy ropes.

The beams and cables ended where a
set of chains fastened their steel
bands to the hands and feet of the
Singer. Each time the great windlass
moved a fraction of an inch,
the tension grew upon the ropes and
left the Singer caught in agony that
grew increasingly unbearable.

Suspended from a rough-hewn crane
there hung a hopper. And everyone
who lived within the ancient city
filed silently along the wall and
dropped a stone within the great
receptacle. The growing weight
increased the stress. The lines groaned
upon the metal bands.

The Keepers of the Ancient Ways
began the execution by laying on
the stones of offense first. It
was their holy stones of accu-
sation that set the great machine
in motion. In fidelity to the
truth, they bowed their knees and

looked to heaven and chanted in
the file of death.

    Oh God of ancient days,
    Thou Keeper of the Ancient Ways,
    Our fathers' God, we praise!

Over and over ran the litany of
death. The weight of accusation
grew with each successive stone.

The Singer seemed small among
the heavy beams of wood. The gray
of the day settled close around the
spiraled towers and by the afternoon,
the fog removed the upper walls from
sight. Still it settled downward.
At last the great machine itself was
shrouded by the mist that came to
cool the fever in the dying Singer.

When the fog had made the city one
great livid criminal, the Singer
looked through glazed eyes and
saw his foe, sitting on an old
and rotten beam. He leered
above the stretched and dying man
before him.

"You give me joy and music you
will never hear, Singer. Groan
for me. Scream the fire that
fills your soul. Spew the venom
of your grudge upon the city.
Never have I known the triumph
of my hate till now."

He rose and walked across the beam
and stepped upon a cable. The added
strain drew the manacles into the

wrists of the dying Singer.

"Check-mate, Singer!" He howled into
the mist and the shrieking of his
laughter was absorbed into the opaque
air.

The Singer felt the agony of dying,
the multiplied pain of a hundred thousand
men all dying at one time.

With an agility of delight the Hater
danced his way around the armature
and strutted on the ropes. He looked
into the fog again and shouted,
"Your move, Earthmaker!"

The great, gray, unseen walls grabbed
the mockery and flung their sonic
echoes from stone to stone. And while
the reverberations rang throughout the
Great Walled City, the Hater in sadistic
gaiety ran out upon the ropes,
swung around a beam and threw
his words outward into the sick sky.

"I have you crying, Earthmaker. You
can never glory in your universal
riches, for I have made you poor. And
there is none to pity you. Everyone
you made has retired to eat and drink
away their absurd holiday, and when
they wake up in the morning their great
machine will have done its work.
You lie at man's caprice and wait for
him to break your heart . . . Earthmaker
is crying at the mercy of his earth.

"You started crying when they broke
his hands. Can it be that the agony

which plunges you in grief can wash
my soul with joy?

"Look how he dies. Cry, Creator, Cry!
This is my day to stand upon the
breast of God and claim my victory
over love. You lost the gamble. In
but an hour your lover will be pulp
upon the gallows. Did you tell him
when his fingers formed the world,
that he would die on Terra, groaning
with his hands crushed and whimpering
in my great machine?"

He laughed and turned to look again
upon the Troubadour.

"Now, who will sing the Father-Spirit's
Song?" he asked the dying man.

The Singer seemed to rally in his
suffering. From somewhere far beyond
himself he drew a final surge
of strength and sang the final verse
again.

"And now the great reduction has begun:
Earthmaker and his Troubadour are one."

He sang. And then his lips fell silently
apart and his head slumped forward
on his chest.

The Father-Spirit wept.

The fog swirled in bleak and utter
numbness.

Existence raved.

The stones bled.

The Shrine of Older Life collapsed
in rubble.

And Terra shuddered in her awful crime.

XXI

Decision is the key to destiny.

"God, can you be merciful and send
me off to hell and lock me in
forever?"

"No, Pilgrim, I will not send you
there, but if you chose to go
there, I could never lock you out."

The Hater cringed to hear the
sound he feared above all else.
The doorway of the worlds stood
open. He felt the giant key
that dangled from his belt. He
wished to gloat a little longer
in his victory but left the
silent gallows where the Singer
was as dead as the rotting beams
of the machine.

He reached the threshold of
eternity and found the doorway
of the worlds not only open but
clearly ripped away. He strained
to hear the everlasting wail, the
eternal dying which he loved.
All was silent. Then he heard
the Song.

"No," he cried. "Give me back
the door and key for this is my
domain." He felt again and found
the great key at his waist had
disappeared.

"Where is the key? Where is the
key?" the Hater cried. But all
the while the Hater knew. Each
man on Terra had a key. And
never could they come into the
Canyon of the Damned unless they
chose to do it. To live there,
men would have to reject the Song.
It was a song that only four
on Terra knew, but it would grow until
the world could sing it.

"Earthmaker, this day was not the
victory I had thought," the World Hater
cried. "We both have lost. You
have lost your Son and I have
lost my kingdom."

It was a hollow loss. Full well
the Hater knew the Canyon of the
Damned would never be as large as
he had hoped.

He steeled himself for the battle
out ahead.

He would have to fight the Song.
He would fight with every
weapon in his arsenal of hate.

But he knew that he would lose.
And he knew that when the course of
time was done, the door would be
put back upon the Canyon of the
Damned, and he would be locked
in with all the discord of the
universe. And he would suffer
with all of those he had taught
to hate the Song or consciously
ignore it.

And he himself would be a prisoner
of the hate he spread on Terra.
And when the doorway of the worlds
was locked the final time, he
himself would be inside the Canyon of
the Damned.

And only God would have the key.

XXII

WHEN GOD LOSES HIS BELOVED
habeas corpus is a weak and futile
law. But Earthlings never seem to
learn that it is futile to dredge
the graveyards for messiahs. No
matter how intently you may man
the cables, the grappling hooks
will always come up empty.

In the morning, the wreckage of the
great machine lay in splintered
beams beneath the wall. It had
fallen in the night. The great iron
pinions that held it to the ancient
stones had given way.

The whole affair had been so wrapped
in mist that none had seen its fall.
But all had heard the roar and crash
of its collapse.

The city had not slept. A common
guilt had kept them thinking of the
man who died above them and the
holiday that they had passed in emptiness.
And when they had tried to sleep, the
image of the Singer etched itself upon
the darkness of the night. They felt
unspoken shame in merely being sons
and grandsons of the masons and
carpenters who had made the great machine
in centuries long gone.

When Terra shuddered in the night, the
old machine had torn itself away and
splintered in a single heap of rotted
wood and rusted iron. And many in the
peaceless night remarked that it was
odd the Singer and the old machine
should die the self-same moment.

Shortly after daybreak the wreckage
lay behind a civil barricade
and a crew of laborers was sent
to clear the chaos from the
streets. A group of men lifted

the heavy beams. Ox-drawn sledges took
them well beyond the city gates.

Each workman feared that he
might be the one to come upon
the mangled body of the Singer who
now lay buried in the last
remains of the machine. The heavy
drayage of debris lasted into early
afternoon.

A workman finally spied the giant
tension cable that drew the heavy
chains. He feared to see the
mutilation he would find beneath
the tangled cables and the ropes.

But when he had pulled the final
chains away, the manacles were empty.
And where the Singer should have
been there lay only a key—a great
key forged from a metal never mined
on earth. When the workman stooped
to pick it up he found that it was
broken. It was clear that whatever door
it might have fit would never see its
use again. That nameless door
would remain forever locked or open. For
a moment the workman wondered which.
"Open," he thought. "Yes, definitely
open."

He pondered the great key. Was it of any
consequence? Should he report it to the
Grand Musician? He finally threw
the broken key into a passing
ox-cart filled with wreckage. He
shrugged his shoulders and set out to
find the overseer.

At length he found the foreman sent to direct the clean-up operation at the wall. "Tell the Grand Musician," he said, "there is no body in the wreckage and the manacles are empty."

XXIII

"What would you like to be when you grow up, little girl?"

"Alive."

The child lay wide awake and
filled with fear. Something dreadful
in the dying of her friend left
her trembling in the cold. To be
an orphan in a world that took
so little thought of homeless
children was tenuous enough. But a
greater dread stalked her smaller
world. The Singer was no more,
and she felt again the way she
had before he came and found her
begging by the roadside.

"Please keep me well," she prayed.
"Father-Spirit, keep me as the
Singer left me." She felt her
little legs to be quite sure they
had not withered in the night.
"Now that he is gone, please,
Father-Spirit," she pled into
the darkness, "must I become
an invalid again?"

In every shadow of the night she saw
the lurking image of the World Hater.
She remembered how he leered at her
and smirked to see her in the
roadside dust. "Oh, Father, it is
better that I had not received
the gift of motion than to have
gained and lost it. I never
can go back again to crawling
in the streets," she sobbed. "Please
do not make me crawl again and
beg. Oh, Father, please . . ."

The first faint coloring of dawn

found her lying in fatigue,
still begging for her legs which
had not suffered any loss for
all her worry. But her agony and doubt
had caused her view of things
to grow narrow in the night.
Even the first pale light of day
did not reveal the world that
really was.

She felt someone beside her on the
simple mat that was her bed.

"You worried about your legs for
nothing," said a voice.

She sat upright in her fear.
In but a moment she was on
her feet and seemed about to run.
Then she looked at him more fully.
Her heart was pumping. "Can it be?"
And she concluded in her madness,
"It is!" She threw herself into
the Singer's arms with such a strong
embrace it all but knocked him over.
"You're alive—alive." She closed
her eyes and opened them to be sure
that blinking would not erase her joy.
"Oh, Singer—I was so afraid. I
thought my legs would be as . . ."

"Yours are better far than mine this
morning," he said.

His hands and feet were barely recog-
nizable. She who had cried for
her own legs was overcome by real
concern for his.

"You healed mine!" she said. "Heal

your own. Please, Singer, make them
well."

"They are well. There is no pain
now."

"But they are scarred and
wounded. How can they be well?"

"Earthmaker leaves the scars, for
they preserve the memory of pain.
He will leave my hands this way
so men will not forget what it can
cost to be a singer in a theater
of hate."

"But the word... the word they
wrote upon your face is gone."

The Singer reached up to his forehead
where the searing iron had left
the accusation of the council.
The word was gone indeed.

"It is," he said, "because Earthmaker
cannot bear a lie. He could not let
me wear the word for He is Truth.
He knows no contradiction in himself.
So learn this, my little friend, no
man may burn a label into flesh and
make it stay when heaven disagrees."

"But did the Father-Spirit agree
with all the other things they did
to your hands and feet?"

"He wished they had not done it...
But, yes... he did agree that without
these wounds Terra could not know
how much he loved her. You will find,

my child, that love rarely ever
reaches out to save except it does
it with a broken hand."

She seemed to understand, and because
he loved her childish eyes so much
he made her ready for the future.

"Do you love me, child?" he asked.

"With all my heart," she answered.

"And would you give me anything I
asked of you?" he said.

"Anything!" she answered.

"It may be hard to give me all I
ask. Not long ago, in the name of
love, I gave you legs. Yesterday
that very love demanded mine. But
the Song is all that matters. It
may be you will have to sing it
where the crowd will shout you
down and demand your legs or life.
But it would be far better to give
them both than to surrender up the
music in your soul. Some will
hate you for the song you love.
They will seek to stop your singing.
But no matter how they treat you,
remember that I suffered everything
before you. And if they should
brand you with a name across
your face..."

"It cannot stay, if heaven disagrees,"
she finished up his statement.

He had stretched her small philosophy.

But he knew that she was growing
in her understanding of the Song.

"Let us stop our talking and say that
for right now it is enough to be a
little girl with two good legs and to
know the sun is shining. Let's go
out into the fields together. Are you
afraid to hold my wounded hand?"
he asked. "It is so ugly."

"It is so beautiful," she disagreed.
He held out his gentle
hand. She placed her little hand
in his and was surprised to
find that when his hand had
closed around her own he had a
healthy grip. "Your hand is firm
and strong. God did not leave it
broken long," she said.

"He never does," he answered.

Hand in hand they walked.
The sunlight brought the brightest
day the world had ever known.
She held his hand as if to
never let him go. She skipped at the
base of her shadow and danced the
way she had the very day they met.

"I'm sorry I had doubts about my
legs," she said, then asked, "Where
are we going?"

"To a man who has some doubts about
his mind."

XXIV

Every constellation is but a
gathering of distant suns. It is
mere perspective that makes
Betelgeuse a star. Seen close
enough she is a raging fire.
A sphere of flaming hydrogen, if it
be nearer, will dominate the sky
and blot out all the lesser lights.
And such a fire will say again,
"Earthmaker has a living Son."

The sunlight came much later to the wall than it did to city streets. Two women hurried through the purple and the silver light of dawn toward the grove where they knew the sentinels had led the Madman. The trees in darkness were menacing and thick. They kept upon the path until the dark and ancient wall towered over them.

"How can we find him in this gloom?" the younger woman asked.

Before the question could be answered, they heard the clanking of his chains. The terrifying sound made them fear him all the more.

"Madman ... please ... we are your friends ... I am the Singer's mother ... I saw you try to save him at the trial ..." Her words fell out in unconnected phrases.

When their eyes had grown accustomed to the light, they found him crumpled like a titan child against the wall. No more a threat.

"Go away," he said, moving very little.

"Please, Madman ... we are your friends. I really am the mother of the man you would have saved."

The other woman said nothing as the
two of them continued. The Madman
said in his despair, "No one could
save him . . . the World Hater won.
He spent the night in laughter
at the gallows."

"I loved my son," the mother said,
"and I must thank you for loving him
as I."

"Yes, I loved him. For one brief day,
my mind was well . . . so short a time. I
knew meaning and reason. But now he's
dead."

"And I with him," she said.

"Today the Hater will be back,"
the Madman said, "with his absurd
pipe. He will play and play until
he leaves me foaming in insanity
again. I'll writhe and wallow
to his joy and die in
hopeless chains."

"We all have chains," at length
the silent woman joined in.
"I too may go back to chains I
thought I'd left for good. When
I try to sing the Ancient Star-Song
the verses are disjointed and
apart."

"I cannot tell how long my mind
will stay when hate returns today,"
sighed the Madman.

The sunlight broke and came at once
above the wall and ran in golden

streams along the blackened stones.
It set the grove aglow with bronze
earth and green wax leaves. The
gray was swallowed up in color and
an oriole sang deep-throated joy.

The three sat in the instant
morning that had baptized them
with suddenness and left them
studying the pathway through the
grove. At the far end, they saw
a little girl walking hand in hand
with a tall man.

On a little knoll of ground just
outside the grove, the stranger
stopped and released the child
and threw his arms into the air
and wrapped a melody in sunlight
and threw the triumph of the morning
against the grove and wall.

"In the beginning was the song of
love," he sang.

The two women were on their feet
within the instant and running
toward the thrilling song that came
with day.

The Madman stood and strained
against his chains. He could not
move, although he threw his massive
weight against the iron that held
him from the Singer. The steel
cut his wrists but did not break.
Then at the zenith of his struggle
he remembered all at once the
principle of reason. He let back
on the chains till they were slack.

"Once more, Lord," he called out
through the trees. "Once more."

Again the Singer lifted up his
bearded head and sang, "In the
beginning was the song of love..."
And through the trees the Madman's
strong sound voice sang back, "And
here's the new redeeming melody, the
only song that can set Terra free."

The chains unlocked themselves and
fell away. The Madman left the dark
and hurried into day.

Like autumn leaves triumph swirled upward
into sky. The song came on forever.

And distant quasars hurrying in
space marveled that the dull and joy-
less world had finally come of age.

Thus Terra joined the universe who
knew the song so long before, when
the parent stars themselves were
tracked by wounded feet. And for
a thousand years the music never
ceased. It ricocheted through
canyons and hung in promise over
all of Terra's seas.

And those who know the Ancient Star-
Song watch with singing for the
sign of footprints in the galaxies
through which the little planet
rides in routine cycles of despair.
But Joy seldom sleeps for long.
And someday in a lonely moment man-
kind will shake an unfamiliar hand
and find it wounded.

THE SINGER

a poetic narrative in the tradition of C. S. Lewis's Narnia Chronicles and J. R. R. Tolkien's Lord of the Rings trilogy—is Calvin Miller's retelling of an age-old story whose significance is unmatched in human history. Those who wish to read it in its original form will find it in the Gospels of Matthew or Mark, Luke or John.

This book is the first of a trilogy which is completed by *The Song* (based on the book of Acts) and *The Finale* (an artistic retelling of the book of Revelation).

Calvin Miller is a graduate of Oklahoma Baptist University and holds the Doctor of Ministries degree from Midwestern Baptist Seminary. He is currently the pastor of a church in Omaha, Nebraska, and is also the author of *Once Upon a Tree, Poems of Protest and Faith, Sixteen Days on a Church Calendar, Burning Bushes and Moon Walks, A Thirst for Meaning, That Elusive Thing Called Joy, Transcendental Hesitation* and *A View from the Fields.*

The cover and interior illustrations are by Joe DeVelasco, a Chicago artist whose innovative work has appeared in many books and magazines.

The Singer is set in 10 point Palatino roman and printed by R. R. Donnelley & Sons Company, The Lakeside Press, Chicago, Illinois and Crawfordsville, Indiana. The cover is printed by Frank Prasil Graphics, Evanston, Illinois.

*Other books in the
Singer Trilogy:
The Song
The Finale
all three available
in a boxed set*